Song of the Mekong River

Written by Na-mi Choi
Illustrated by Sinae Jo
Edited by Joy Cowley

big & SMALL

At dawn the rooster crows
and wakes up the people.
Soon boats will appear on the water,
big fishing boats with nets
and boats on their way to the markets.
Morning is coming to the Mekong River.

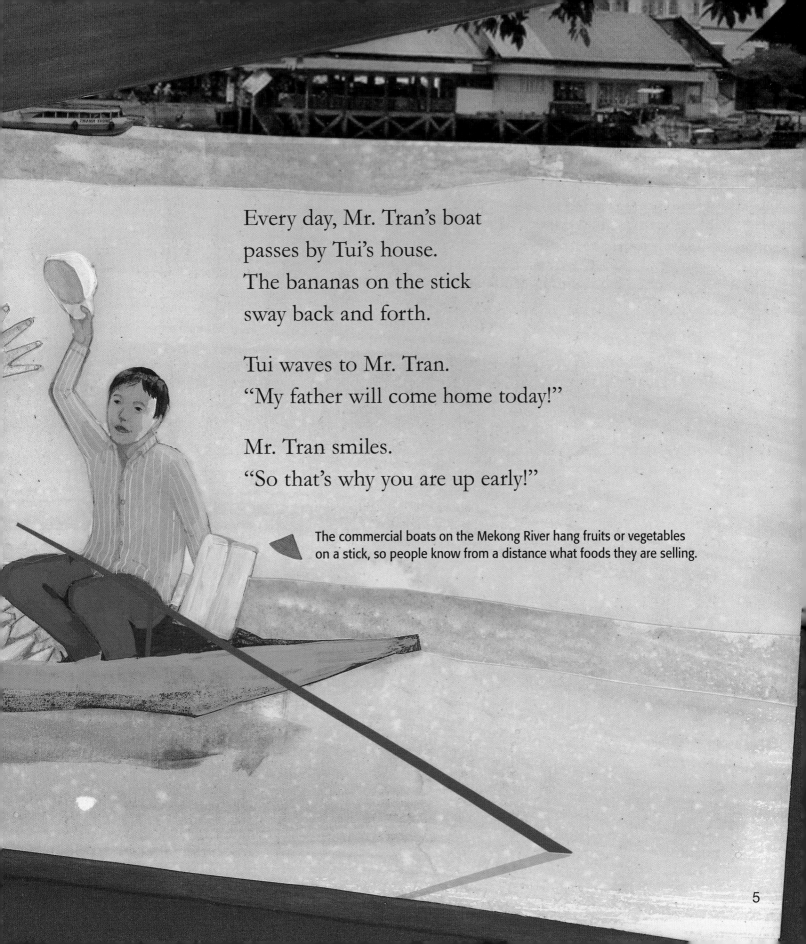

Every day, Mr. Tran's boat
passes by Tui's house.
The bananas on the stick
sway back and forth.

Tui waves to Mr. Tran.
"My father will come home today!"

Mr. Tran smiles.
"So that's why you are up early!"

The commercial boats on the Mekong River hang fruits or vegetables
on a stick, so people know from a distance what foods they are selling.

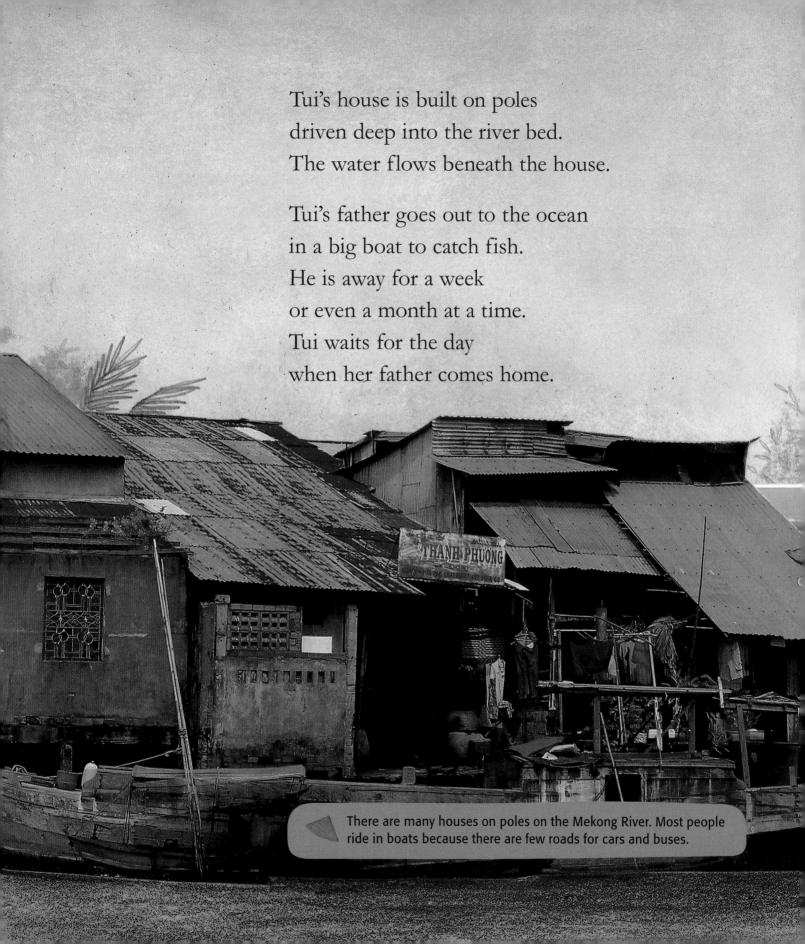

Tui's house is built on poles
driven deep into the river bed.
The water flows beneath the house.

Tui's father goes out to the ocean
in a big boat to catch fish.
He is away for a week
or even a month at a time.
Tui waits for the day
when her father comes home.

There are many houses on poles on the Mekong River. Most people ride in boats because there are few roads for cars and buses.

Tui's mother is busy loading her boat
with fruits for the water market.
Tui asks her, "How far away
do you think Dad's boat is?"

"He is still out at sea,"
replies her mother.

 There are water markets in many parts of the Mekong River,
where boats gather to buy and sell items.

Tui's mother has a supermarket boat.
Other boats sell noodles or rice
or items, like kitchenware
and building supplies.
Tourists travel on some boats,
and there are boats
that are houses for families.

The sun shines on the Mekong River.
Tui's friends wave to her and say,
"Our boat is going to the Pacific Ocean!"
But Tui doesn't want to play.
She is waiting for her father.

Tui's grandmother wants to buy flowers
for the altars at Tui's house.
The flowers need to be fresh
because they are gifts for ancestors.

 Vietnamese people have altars for ancestors in their houses. Every morning
they burn incense, offer flowers and fruit, and pray for their family.

Tui and her grandmother
get on Ms. Trang's boat.
Ms. Trang works as a transporter
for traveling customers.
Many waterways are narrow
and not all boats can travel in them.
Ms. Trang drops them off
close to the markets.

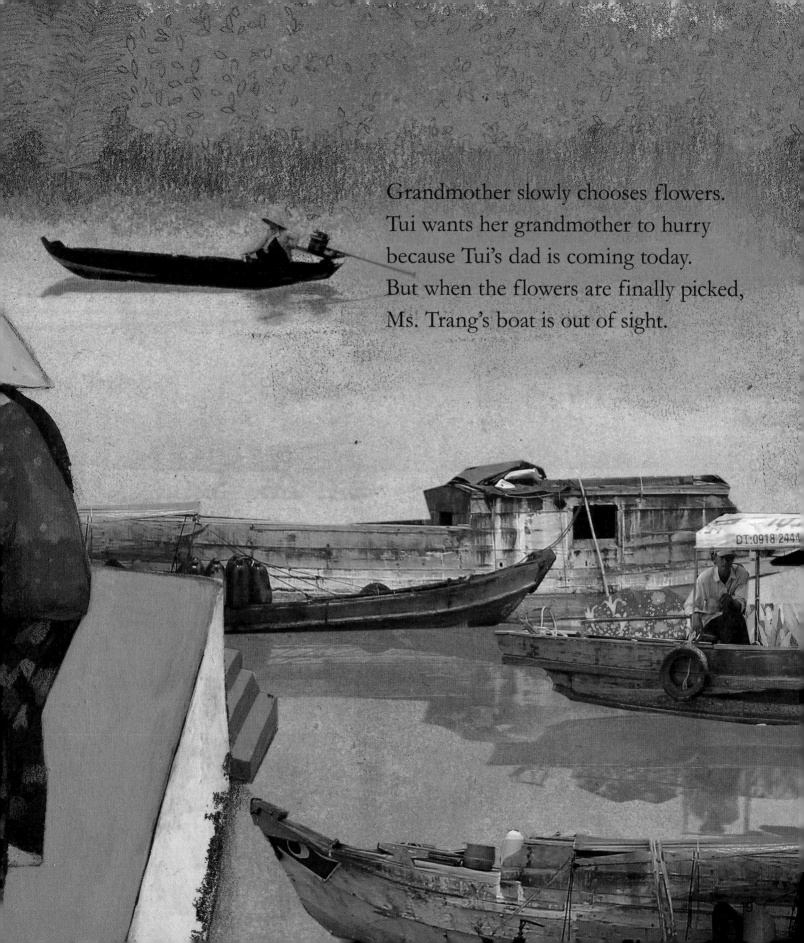

Grandmother slowly chooses flowers.
Tui wants her grandmother to hurry
because Tui's dad is coming today.
But when the flowers are finally picked,
Ms. Trang's boat is out of sight.

At last Tui sees Ms. Trang's boat
and she and Grandmother climb aboard.
Tui says, "Dad will get home before we do
if Ms. Trang doesn't go faster."

Tui asked Ms. Trang to hurry
but she rows as slowly as usual.

It is nearly evening
but the breeze is still warm.
Big and small boats go past
and Tui wants to cry.
Will they never get home?

22

At last, Tui's house can be seen.
"Hey, Tui! Hey, Tui!"

Tui's father has seen her
on Ms. Trang's boat
and he is waving and yelling.

Tui forgets about crying.
"Daddy! Daddy!" she yells.

About Vietnam
Vietnam and the Mekong River

The Vietnamese flag is red with a yellow star. The flag was adopted as the national flag in 1976 when the country was united. Red represents the revolution and the struggle for independence, and the five corners of the yellow star symbolize the solidarity of laborers, farmers, intellectuals, youths and soldiers respectively.

Mekong, the Biggest River in South East Asia

The Mekong River is one of the longest rivers in the world. It starts in the Tibetan region in China and flows through Laos, Thailand and Cambodia to Vietnam. Many Vietnamese build houses on the rivers. Most live close to the Huong River in the northern region and the Mekong River in the south. Because there are not many roads, people usually travel by boats on the rivers and their tributaries.

Houses on the Mekong River

The Prosperous Mekong Delta

At the mouth of the Mekong River is fertile land where crops grow well. This is called the Mekong Delta. Due to warm weather and the rich soil brought down from the river, farmers are able to harvest three times a year. The rice grown in the Mekong Delta is more than enough to feed the entire Vietnamese population. This is why the Mekong Delta is called "the storehouse of Vietnam." Vietnam is one of the three major exporters of rice – along with Thailand and the USA.

Farmers working on the Mekong Delta plains

Nón lá and áo dài

Tui's mother was wearing a cone shaped hat called nón lá. It is usually
made out of palm leaves and people wear it for protection from the strong
sunlight. Ào dài is a Vietnamese national costume for women. It consists
of a long tight-fitting tunic and wide pants, comfortable when riding a bike.
Young woman wear white or light-colored áo dài, and married or older
women wear vivid colors.

Markets on the River

The water markets on the Mekong River are remarkably large.
Hundreds of boats come in and out of the markets every day to sell things.
Besides fish, there are agricultural products and livestock such as chickens,
ducks and pigs. Some boats make food and sell it to other boats,
and of course, there are passenger boats like Ms. Trang's.

Country with a Painful History

Vietnam has often been invaded by strong countries. In ancient times it was governed by China, and until 1954 it was a colony of France. After the French left, Vietnam was divided into two states, North and South Vietnam. A long war was fought between the two sides and many other countries became involved. The war ended in 1975, and the country was united. Although the Vietnamese people endured lots of suffering from the long war, they are proud of their unification.

Vietnam Military History Museum in Hanoi

Vietnamese Fishing Boats

Vietnamese fishing boats, like Tui's dad's in the story, are still mostly constructed of wood and run on diesel engines. They must be carefully maintained as they are often out to sea for a month, and they travel up to 250 miles offshore. It can be very dangerous as communication equipment is poor, so they do not know when bad weather is approaching. The boats are often owned by families and they provide income for the household.

Vietnamese fishing boats in harbor

Fish caught at sea are sold in fish markets.

The Heaven of Food

Three-quarters of Vietnam consists of mountain and the rest is rich flat land alongside the rivers. The Huong River and the Mekong River flow through Vietnam and to the east is the ocean. Thanks to the diversity of the terrain, not only rice, but also potatoes, coconuts and coffee are produced. People catch a variety of fish in the rivers and ocean – including lobster, shrimp and squid. Because of this abundance, Vietnam is known as the "heaven of food." Pho is a typical Vietnamese dish consisting of noodles made of rice, with hot meat soup.

Pho is often eaten at breakfast in Vietnam.

Halong Bay, Nature's Work of Art

In the northern part of Vietnam, there is Halong Bay made up of about 1,600 big and small islands and limestone pillars. The rocks have been eroded over a long time, to form interesting shapes. Although no humans live on these islands, they are inhabited by animals and plants. "Halong" means "descent of the dragon." The name comes from a myth that precious stones and pearls were spat out of a dragon to keep invaders from coming across the sea.

Halong Bay

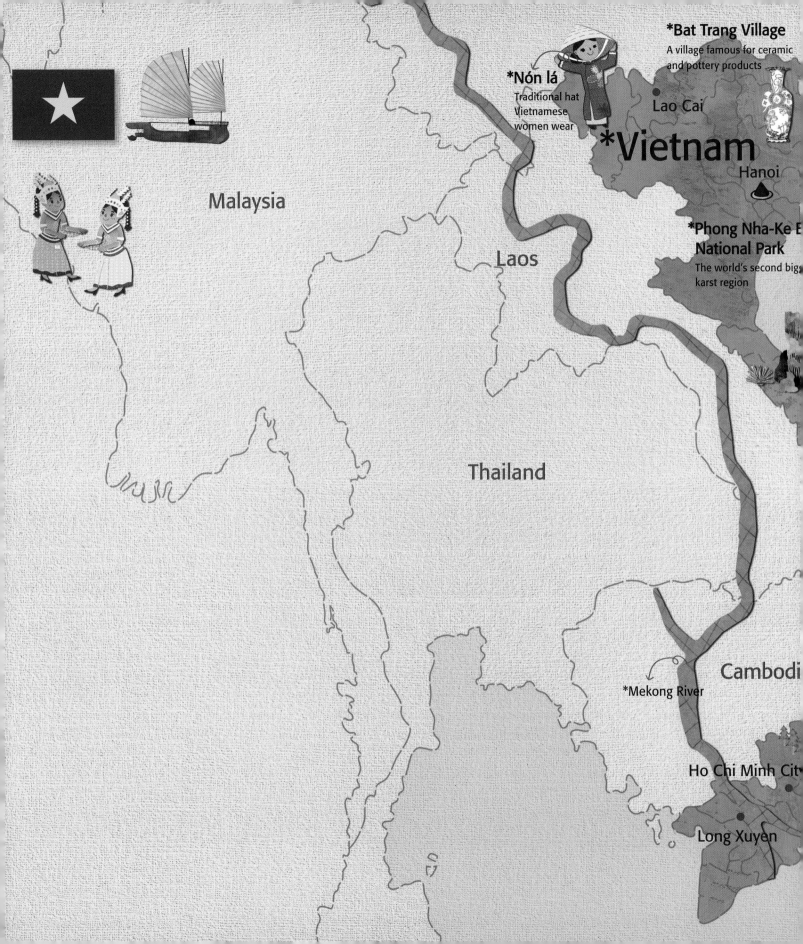

Malaysia

Laos

Thailand

*Nón lá
Traditional hat
Vietnamese
women wear

*Bat Trang Village
A village famous for ceramic
and pottery products

Lao Cai

*Vietnam

Hanoi

***Phong Nha-Ke E
National Park**
The world's second big
karst region

*Mekong River

Cambodi

Ho Chi Minh City

Long Xuyen

China

*Ha Long Bay
A UNESCO World Heritage site
that features over 1600 karst isles

Nang

*Motorcycle
The main form of transportation
in Vietnam, along with bicycles

*Pho
Vietnamese rice noodle

Nha Trang

War Remnants Museum
A war museum where weapons and documents
from the Vietnam War are displayed

Vietnam

Name: Socialist Republic of Vietnam

Location: North-east of Indochina Peninsula

Area: 127,247 mi^2 (329,659 km^2)

Capital: Hanoi

Population: 89.71 million (2013)

Religion: Indigenous religions, Buddhism

Main Exports: Crude oil, rice, coffee,
marine products, textiles, coal

South China Sea

Original Korean text by Na-mi Choi
Illustrations by Sinae Jo
Korean edition © Aram Publishing

This English edition published by big & SMALL in 2015
by arrangement with Aram Publishing
English text edited by Joy Cowley
English edition © big & SMALL 2015

Distributed in the United States and Canada by
Lerner Publishing Group, Inc.
241 First Avenue North
Minneapolis, MN 55401 U.S.A.
www.lernerbooks.com

Photo attributions by page - left to right, top to bottom
Pages 26: public domain; © Wayne77 (CC-BY-SA-3.0); © Quốc Anh Võ
(Own work) (CC BY-SA 3.0); Page 27: © Doran (CC-BY-SA-3.0); Page 28:
public domain; © Lucas Jans (CC BY-SA 2.0); © Lucas Jans (CC BY-SA 2.0);
Page 29: © David McKelvey (CC-BY-2.0); © Lawrence Murray (CC-BY-2.0)

ISBN: 978-1-925233-52-0

Printed in the United States of America
1 – CG – 5/31/15